THE FORBES FAMILY HISTORY

Scotland to West Tennessee

By

Katherine Fletcher

THE FORBES FAMILY HISTORY

This FORBES family starts in 1100 Scotland and goes to Pennsylvania, South Carolina and Memphis, Tennessee. They migrated to America in the 1740's. Join me in discovering 26 generations on this Forbes family line.

This history is full of interesting Revolutionary War soldiers, a story of a scalping by Indians and real Scottish royalty who lived in real castles.

The name Forbes comes from the lands of Donside, the southern part of the Pictish kingdom. It comes from the Gaelic word Forba, meaning field. Forbeses were known as the Forbais. A charter was given to the family by King Alexander III who died in 1286. Duncan Forbes was one of the first. Sir Alexander Forbes (above) married a granddaughter of King Robert III.

Here is the Forbes Clan Badge from Scotland

Forbes Plant Badge   BROOM

FORBES TARTAN COLORS

GENERATION ONE

John Altha Turnage (1865-1959) and Mittie Florence George (1874-1942)

John died in Symington, TN.   Mittie died in Tipton, TN.

They owned a large farm in Burlison.

Children:

Mary Agnes (1894-1966) married Hilliard Jessie Murphy Sr.

Gracie Elizabeth Turnage, b. 1899, d. 1987 married Sherod Bowers

Earldon R Turnage, b. 23 May 1914-1984

Ivie Myrtle 1904-1998 married Harold C. Fletcher * This is the author's grandmother

 Lydie L Turnage, b. 1900, Tipton, TN, USA

Anne Pearl Turnage, b. Jun 1897-1975 / married James McClerkin (Calvin)

Bernice

Cloudy

Lottie (1902) married Orville Hayden

Bejamin Martin 1892-1950 married Berta Belle Draffin

Mary (Maddie) Agnes 1894-

Eslie M. 1909- married Milton Glydewell

Donnia Altha 1895-1897

Claude Clifton 1898-1899

GENERATION TWO

John George (1885-1930) and Margaret Forbess (1851-1928).

Born and died in Tipton, TN

Their children:

James Onvie   1885-1978

Asa Gorforth   1880-1969

Fannie May 1884-1939

Minnie Allie 1878-1942

Annie Demetra 1871-1952

Lillie   1889-

Mittie (1873-1942)   married John Altha Turnage

John Altha Turnage and Mittie George

Mittie George Turnage at her farm

GENERATION THREE

Thomas J. Forbess (1821-1863) and Mary Catherine Goforth (1813-1899).

Margaret Goforth's picture

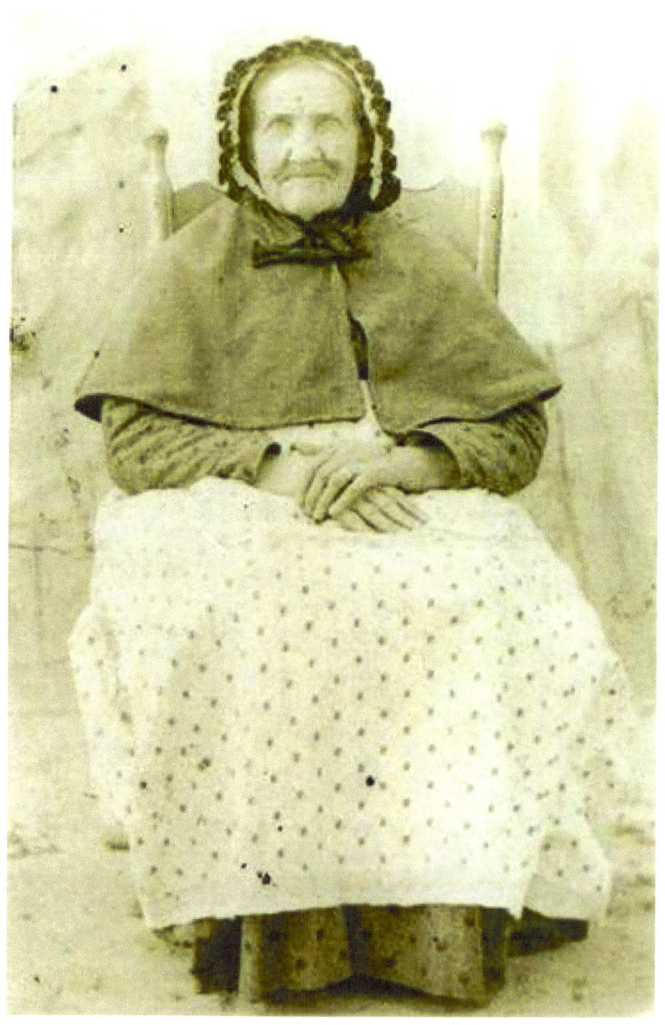

Their children:

John Asbury – 1854-1932 Tipton Co, TN / married Fannie Griggs
– this is the line of my uncle Woodrow Forbes line . John's son
was Joseph Edward who married Bertha Davidson. Their son
was Joseph Woodrow who was married to Katie Proctor.

Solomon Roan 1849-1933 married Florence Forbas

Jim (James M) 1841-1922 married Margurite E. Bettie

Here is Jim's picture

Thomas Jefferson Jr. 1844-1927 married 3 x Joanna Miller, Mary Lusina Delancy,   He fought in the civil war.

Sarah Ann 1855-1935 married Washington Joyner

Asa L 1839=1919   married Penelope Ann McCraw

Mary Elizabeth 1847-1904 married William Henry Joyner – this Joyner family is also related to me on the Fletcher side.

Margaret married John George

Malinda E 1858-1867 died at age 9 Milanda's dress caught fire while burning off a corn field. Her brother john caught her, but she pulled away and ran and died.

This is Jim's (James Monroe's) house in Simonton, Tenn - on the hill across from Richard Turnage's home

Back Row (adults) L to R: Amanda Barnes, Olivia Forbess, Babe in arms is Vergie, James Forbess, Sarah Forbess, Kate Forbess Millican. The Children, front row (not sure who is who) Selma Forbess, Edna Forbess, Clarence Forbess, Richard Forbess, Ila Millican. (I think Ila is the one with the white flower on her left shoulder) Also named is Alice Gillihan

Jim fought in the war

Feb. 14, 1903 Confederate Soldiers Pension Application
A Private of Company H., 51st TN Inf. C.S.A also known as Captain Shelton's Co., 51st TN Inf.

Enlisted 1862 captured at Marietta, GA on July 5, 1864 and a prisoner of war at Camp Morton, Indianapolis, Indiana. Released on oath May 20, 1865.

Residence of Brighton, Tipton Co, TN. Family consist of "Self and

Wife 60 years old, 2 boys and 3 girls all grown and married. My daughter is a widow and her 5 year old girl lives with us. I was born 1841 in Tipton Co, TN. I run a small saw mill and I farm a few acres of land."

GENERATION FOUR

Archibald Barron Forbess (1795-1850) and Margaret Catherine Hutchinson (1799-1853).

Archibald was born in Rock Hill, York, South Carolina and died in De Soto, Mississippi.   He was in the war of 1812 and fought against the Seminole Indians.

He married in 1817.

Their children:

John Calvin (1819-1904) married Mary William Howell born in York, SC and died Loanoke, AK,

Margaret C. (1819-1847)

Thomas Jefferson (1821-1863) married Mary Catherine Goforth –part of my Uncle Woodrow's line.

Samuel Hutchinson (1823-1877) married Rhoda Dueast – lived in Davidson and Tipton Co, TN. Sam was a blacksmith and at age 24 was convicted of murder in the 2nd degree and sentenced to 15 years to jail. He was discharged 1854 by a pardon. Samuel stabbed with a knife a Martin S. Goldsby.

Rhoda (1825-1847) married William Dempsey

Archibald Barney (1827-1905) married Sarah Ann ?

Mary Isabella (1830-1898)

Rebecca Ann (1832-

William Flannigan (1837-1914) married Mary Elizabeth Payne

James Perry (1840-)

HERE IS ARCHIBALD'S MIGRATION STORY TO TENNESSEE

"This family lived the first 17 years or so of their married life in York County, South Carolina. Like so many York County residents who had been plagued by years of droughts and bad crops, this couple wanted and sought out a new life. Thelma Forbes Duke continues their story in her article:From the Duke Article:

".....They came to Tipton County,Tennessee in a wagon train with the people that started Salem A. R. P. Church there in 1837. Archibald's was the only Forbes family listed on the Tipton County 1840 Census. Archibald served in the 1st regiment (Means') South Carolina Militia in the War of 1812. He enlisted for 6 months on 1 September 1814 and discharged 1 Mar 1815. He lived in Tipton County until about 1848 when he moved his family to Northern Mississippi after losing his land in Tipton County in a law suit with George Patton. He filed for bounty land, on the "act passed by the United States, 28th September 1850" - bounty land to certain officers and soldiers who had been engaged in the military service. He died before his 80 acres was awarded. Due to a lawsuit of his minor children about this land, I was able to establish parentage to my Thomas."

"The 1837 Tax Roll in District 8 shows Archibald Forbes had 171 acres with a value of $588. By 1838, Archibald Forbes owned 220 acres of land with a value of $1,370.

Tipton County and DeSoto County have been the focus of migration for several Hutchison family groups. Margaret C. Hutchison Forbes' sister, Rhoda Hutchinson Reid, stayed here for 6-7 years before going to DeSoto County and fimal settlement in Bastrop County, Texas. Sister Cynthia Hutchison Thompson, Harris's stepfamily, the Wrights and Paynes, had settled in Tipton County about the same time as the Forbes family. A few years later, her brother, John, brought his family from DeSoto County, Mississippi.Of course, Archibald and Margaret C. Forbes later moved to DeSoto County. Brother Alfred R. Hutchinson has made his home there for 15 years or so before the Forbes family arrival. There were many York County residents now living in DeSoto County at the time." (Source: "Descendents of John and Sarah Hutchison", Hutch(er)son Research Group)

Archibald married again to Sterling Harris Pinner

Notes for STERLING HARRIS PINNER:
1896 His 2nd wife Eliza Ann (Yount) Pinner filed for a Widow's Pension.
Her comments: "I never new Sterling until after his services in the Florida War with the Seminole Indians and know nothing of his
service...when I first bacame aquianted with him he was 5 ft 10 in,   complexion fair, eyes blue, light hair or sand colored and weighed 135 pounds"

Military service: Seminole Indians 1836, 1837

GENERATION FIVE

John Forbes (1752-1829) and Rebecca Barron (1762-1853)

John was born in Pennsylvania and died in Rock Hill, SC.

Rebecca Baron was born in Antrim, Ireland and died in Portland Mills, Parke, Indiana. Her parents were Archibald Barron (1737-1817) and Elizabeth Ingram (1735-1809). Her father served in the Revolutionary War in the SC Militia and was a wagon master.

Grave of Archibald Barron – Rebecca's father.

John also served in the Revolutionary War and there is a Sons of the American Revolution applications on file.

Forbes, John, R3645

d 24 Oct 1829

m. Rebecca Barron, 1780

While a resident of York District, he served three hundred fifty-two days during 1780, 1781, and 1782 of which sixty days was as a lieutenant of foot under Capt. Moffett and Col. Samuel Watson, one hundred ninety-seven days as a lieutenant of horse under Col Hill and twenty-four days as a horseman under Gen Sumter of the Quarter House. In addition, he served forty-five days as a foot soldier under Gen. Henderson and ten other days under officers unknown. He was wounded in the engagement at Williamson's Plantation. C.D. A. A. 2459: R445.

Here's a copy of John's pension record talking about his war injuries

Pension records Nov 15, 1819 for John Forbes.
---(begin transcription)---
Upon examining the wounds of Mr. John Forbis Senior, I believe them to render him partially incapable of making a compentant support for himself and family who are dependant upon his exertions, his extream age taken into consideration with the balance of his wounds renders him more incapable of that to make a substance.

Nov 15 1819 Ed Jennings
Surgt. of 12 Regiment
of Militia

South Carolina
York District

Personally came Joseph Forbis before me who being duly sworn made oath in due form of how that he is a brother of John Forbis and that said John Forbis was a military soldier under Colonal Neal in the Revolutionary War that he was Literally cut to pieces and wounded in such a manner that he was entirely unable to make a support for himself and family and that by his wounds now in his old age renders him incapable of making a sufficient support for his family who dependance is on him. Also came Captain Joseph McCorkle and Mary Smith who on oath saith that they were personally acquainted with John Forbis in the Revolutionary War and that the above afidavit is true as they were frequently with the said John Forbis. Sworn to and subscribed before me this 16th day of November 1819.

Elias Robertson, JP Joseph Forbis

Joseph McCorkle
Mary (x) Smith her mark

STORY OF JOHN FORBESS AND SCALPING

I came across a story about John Forbess during the war and how he was saved by a women named Prudence. John had been scalped by Indians and left to die. Prudence had a number of milking cows out in her pasture in York, SC and one of the cows didn't come back that night. She went out to the woods to find the cow and she heard someone moaning. She found John laying in water. She rode off to get help and John was rescued and nursed back to life.

Harriet Prudence Pattherson was an interesting woman during the Revolutionary War. She married John Hall. They built a trading post in York, Sc after migrating from Charleston, SC. She rode to Charleston under the guise of getting medicine but in fact would gather information and pass it along to the American army. The British discovered this and hated her. She also rode her horse to other towns for salt supplies.

JOHN AND REBECCA - They married in 1780 in York, SC.

Grave of John Forbes

Grave of Rebecca Forbes

Their children:

Elizabeth "Betsy" (1783) married William Shaw

Margaret (1784-

Rebecca (1786-

Sarah Sally (1788-1830) married Daniel Shaw

Ann (1790-1853)

Rachel (1791-1830) married Benjamin Jones

John (1793-1856) married Ann Shaw

Archibald Barron (1795-1850)

Prudence (1797-1805) died at 7 years old.

Thomas (1801-1868) married Sarah H. Sally McCorkle

Tabitha (1804-1883) married Alexander Harbinson

Arthur   (1806-1888) married Eliza B. Hutchinson

Bible Record of John Forbes

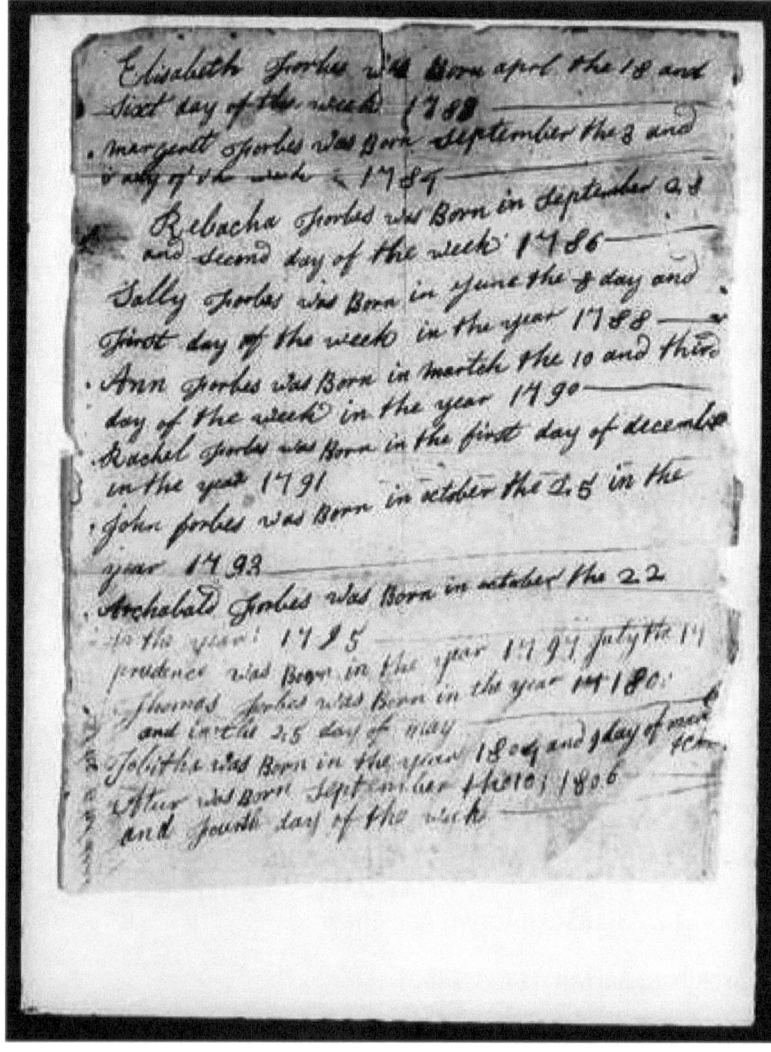

Source: F.P.A. No. R.3645 Rebecca Forbes, Widow of John
Forbes, South Carolina soldier, 04 July 1836 [The heirs of John &
Rebecca Forbes attempted to obtain a pension for their father's
Revolutionary War service after their mother died in 1834.
Thomas Forbes, a son in Parke County, Indiana, had the Forbes
family Bible and sent the attached family record from it to
South Carolina and it was then sent to Washington, DC, 14
October 1847.] [No title page, publication date or place or
marriage record.] [Only the Family Record of the children's
births has survived.] [Thelma Forbess Duke note 26 Feb 1993: I
have Arthur born 9th Sept 1806; John Jr. states in another
document (John Jr.'s own family Bible record) that he was born
26 October 1794.]

GENERATION SIX

Joseph Forbes (1730-1801) and Elizabeth McCorkle (1716-1794)

Joseph was born in Pennsylvania and died in Rock Hill, SC. His
name is also shown as Forbus.

In 1762 he lived in Pitt County, NC.

Elizabeth McCorkle was born in Scotland and died in Rock Hill,
SC. Her father is William MacCorkle born 1690 in Argyllshire,
Scotland.

Joseph also served in the Revolutionary War.

From Roster of South Carolina Patriots in the American
Revolution found on Ancestry.

Forbes, Joseph (b. Pa. -d. 2 October 1829) He entered service
during the fall of 1778 in the Old York District and served under
Col. Neel, Capt. Low and Lt. Barry and marched to the frontiers
of Georgia. During December 1777 (1779?), he was drafted to

serve under Capt. Bluf, Lt. Bluf, Lt fabber, and Col. Watson and was sent to Charleston. He re-enlisted during May 1780 to serve under Capt. B. Thompson, Lt Forbys, Col. Neel and Gen. Sumter. This unit marched to N.C. and back to S. C. after Tories. Thereafter, he was in Sumter's Defeat and was discharged on 17 August. During October 1780, he re-enlisted to serve under Capt. Moffett, Lt. Moore, and Col. Hampton and marched to Hillsboro, N.C., to Newberry, S.C., to Guilford, N.C., to Henry Courthouse, Va, and back home, where he was discharged during March 1781.

Elizabeth Forbes

Their children:

Ann Forbes (1744-1798)

Arthur Forbes (1748-1823) born in Pitt, NC

John Forbes (1752-1829)

Joseph Forbes (1755-1833) born in Philadelphia, died in Rutherford Co, NC.

GENERATION SEVEN

Nathanel Forbes (1700-) and Isabella Stewart (1700-)

Born in Scotland – died in Pennsylvania

Isabella was also born in Drumin, Scotland.

Their children:

John

Joseph 1730-1801

GENERATION EIGHT

William Forbes (1660-1715) and Agnes Forbes (1674-)

William was born in Aberdeenshire, Scotland

He was married multiple times.

Wife Agnes Forbes (1674) from Newe, Aberdeenshire, Scotland

Children:

 Nathanel Forbes (1700_) and

Hugh Forbes (1705-1769)

GENERATION NINE

John Forbes (1645-1712) and Margaret Arbuthnot (1642)

Birth 1645 in Monymusk, Aberdeenshire, Scotland
Death 1712 in Christ Church, Middlesex, Virginia, United
States

Sir John Forbes of Monymusk

Margaret Arbuthnot

>   Birth 1642 in Arbuthnott, Kincardineshire, Scotland
>   Death

, Hon. Margaret Arbuthnott, daughter of <u>Robert Arbuthnott,</u> 1st Viscount of Arbuthnott and Lady Marjory Carnegie

John married Barbara Delmahoy in 1678 in Scotland
He arrived in Virginia in 1682 at age 37.   Records show he married again at Christ Church, VA in 1686 to Mary Mills Shipley.   Unsure when he married Margaret Arbuthnot.

Children with Barbara: Barbara is from Cheshire, England, she died 1710

John Forbes (1680-1716)
Agnus (1684)
John Purvis (1686-1740)

Barbara (1688-)

Children with Mary Mills Shippey:

Jane Forbes (1657-1696)

Children with Margaret Arbuthnot

William (1660-1715)

GENERATION TEN

William Forbes (1601-1676) and Jane Burnett (1603-1677)

> William was born in Birth 4 Sep 1601 in Monymusk, Aberdeenshire, Scotland

> Death 11 Jun 1676 in Monymusk, Aberdeenshire, Scotland

Their children:

John Forbes (1645-1712)

daughter

GENERATION ELEVEN

William Forbes (1575-1661) and Elizabeth Wishart (1577-)

> Birth 1575 in Monymusk, Aberdeenshire, Scotland
> Death 22 Jul 1661 in Monymusk, Aberdeenshire, Scotland

Elizabeth Wishart

>Birth 1577 in Aberdeenshire, Scotland
>Death

Elizabeth's parents are John Wishart (1540) and Jean Douglas (1545)

Their children:

William (1601-1676)

GENERATION TWELVE

William Forbes (1531-1618) and Margaret Douglas (1551)

>Birth 1531 in Monymusk, Aberdeenshire, Scotland
>Death 1618

Margaret Douglas

>Birth 1551 in Dumfries-shire, Scotland
>Death in Scotland

Margaret's parents are James Douglas (1507-1575) and Christian Montgomerie (1520-1575)

GENERATION THIRTEEN

Duncan Forbes (1505-1587) and Agnes Gray (1511)

>Birth 1505 in Monymusk, Aberdeenshire, Scotland
>Death 1587 in Aberdeenshire, Scotland

Agnes Gray

> Birth 1511 in Aberdeen, Aberdeenshire, Scotland
> Death

Children:

William 1531-1618

Elizabeth

GENERATION FOURTEEN

William Forbes (1478-1560) and Margaret Lumsden (1483-1560)

> Birth 1478 in Corsendae, Aberdeen, Scotland
> Death bef 1560 in Corsendae, Aberdeen, Scotland

Margaret

> Birth 1483 in Cushnie, Aberdeenshire, Scotland
> Death bef 1560 in Monymusk, Aberdeenshire, Scotland

Margaret's parents were Thomas Lumsden and Marjory Gordon.

Children:

Duncan

James

GENERATION FIFTEEN

Duncan Forbes (1444-1510) and Christian Mercer (1449-1490)

>Birth abt 1444 in Monymusk Corsindae Monymusk,
>Aberdeenshire, Scotland
>Death 1510 in Monymusk Corsindae Monymusk,
>Aberdeenshire, Scotland

Christian Mercer

>Birth abt 1449 in Corsendae, Aberdeenshire, Scotland
>Death abt 1490 in Corse, Aberdeenshsire, Scotland

GENERATION SIXTEEN

James 2nd Lord Forbes (1424-1460) and Gille Egidia Keith (1424-1473)

>Birth 1424 in Forbes Castle, Aberdeenshire, Scotland
>Death 30 Sep 1460 in Forcalquier Castle, Alpes De Haute
>Provence, Provence, France

Gille Egidia Keith

>Birth 1424 in Forbes Castle, Aberdeenshire, Scotland
>Death 14 Aug 1473 in Forcalquier Castle, Alpes De
>Haute Provence, Provence, France

Gille's parents are Sir William Earl of Marischal Scotland Keith (138901464) and Mary Lady Hamilton (1400-1442) . They lived Dunottar Castle, Kincardineshire, Scotland. Lady Mary Hamilton lived Cadzow Castle, Lanarkshire, Scotland.

Their children:

William Gray Willie Forbes (1442-1473)

William Lord Forbes (1442-1483)

Duncan Forbes (1444-1510)

GENERATION SEVENTEEN

Alexander (1rst Lord Forbes) Forbes (1377-1448) and Lady Elizabeth Mary of Angus, BoF Douglas (1398-1460)

> Birth 20 Jun 1377 in Forbes Castle, Aberdeenshire, Scotland
> Death 16 Oct 1448 in Forbes Castle, Aberdeenshire, Scotland

He fought in the Battle of Beaugé in 1421, in the Scots contingent of the French Army.[2] On 16 October 1423 he had charter of the lands of Forbes.

He also married Lady mary Stewart in 1423.

Lady Elizabeth

> Birth 24 Feb 1398 in Mar Castle, Aberdeenshire, Scotland
> Death 1460 in Yester Castle, Gifford, East Lothian, Scotland

FROM WIKIPEDIA:

Alexander de Forbes, 1st Lord Forbes (c. 1380 - 1448), also feudal baron of Forbes, was a Scottish peer.

He was the eldest son of Sir Alexander de Forbes (d. 1405), Justiciary of Aberdeen, and Coroner of that county, by his wife, a daughter of Kennedy of Dunure.

Alexander de Forbes fought at the Battle of Harlaw in 1411, and appears among the Scottish forces sent to the assistance of Charles, Dauphin of France, afterwards King Charles VII, and had a share in the victory obtained over the English at Beauge, in Anjou, on March 22, 1424. But soon after, at the desire of King James I of Scotland, then a prisoner in England, Forbes quit the French service and subsequently obtained three Safe-conducts at different times to visit England, with one hundred persons in his retinue each time, to wait upon his sovereign, James I.

He was created a Lord of Parliament sometime after 1436. The precise date of the peerage creation is not known (although Brown gives 1440), but in a precept, dated July 12, 1442, he is already styled Lord Forbes.

The first Lord Forbes married Lady Elizabeth (or Mary), only daughter of George Douglas, earl of Angus, a granddaughter of King Robert II of Scotland, by whom he had two sons and three daughters. He was succeeded by his eldest son:

James Forbes, 2nd Lord Forbes, (d. c. 1460).

Her parents are Sir George Douglas (1376-1402) and Lady mary Douglas Kennedy GE Stewart (1380-1458) . Sir George Birth 1376 in Mar, Aberdeenshire, Scotland/Death 1402 in Battle Of Homildon Hill, Scotland. Lady Mary Birth 1380 in Isle of Bute, Ayrshire, Scotland / Death 1458 in Strathblane Castle, Stirlingshire, Scotland

Here's some more information about Lady Douglas Kennedy :

> Lady mary Stewart is the daughter of Robert III Stewart, King of Scotland and mother Annabel Drummond. She

married by contract George Douglas, 1rst Earl of Angus. She married secondly Sir James Kennedy. She married third Sir William Graham. She married fourthly Sir William Edmonstone. Lady Mary Stewart gained the title of Princess Mary of Scotland.

Lady Mary and Alexander Forbes children:

Alexander Fyvie Meldrum (1406-1448)

Annabella

William

Margaret

Marion Elizabeth Forbes (1412-)

James 2nd Lord Forbes (1424-1460)

GENERATION EIGHTEEN

Sir John with Black Lips Forbes (1332-1406) and Elizabeth Margaret Kennedy (1336-1375)

> Birth 1332 in Forbes Castle, Aberdeenshire, Scotland
> Death 20 Nov 1406 in Forbes, Aberdeenshire, Scotland

Sir John was Justiciary and Coroner of Aberdeenshire. He was invested as a Knight before 6 April 1391.

Elizabeth Kennedy

> Birth 1336 in Maybole, Ayrshire, Scotland
> Death 1375 in Forbes Castle, Aberdeenshire, Scotland

Her parents are John Kennedy (1316-1385) and Mary DeCarrick (1310-1400) . They were from Maybole, Ayrshire. Her grandparents are Gilbert Kennedy (1300-1385) and Lady Agnes Maxwell Baroness (1291-1345). Gilbert died in Trabzon, Turkey. Lady Agnes was from East Kilbride, Lanarkshire, Scotland.

Children:

Malcolm Forbes   1360 – 1448
Duncan Evil Forbes   1362 – 1406
John Forbes 1362 – 1404
Alexander (1st Lord Forbes) Forbes 1377 – 1448
Laird William Forbes Kinaldy 1382 – 1445
John Laird Tolquhon Forbes   1384 – 1453
Alaster Cam Brux Forbes 1386 – 1466
Laird William Forbes Kinaldy 1386 – 1466

GENERATION NINETEEN

John DeForbes (1302-1331) and Margaret Lord (1311-1349)

> Birth 1302 in Forbes, Aberdeenshire, Scotland
> Death 1331 in Duplin, Ayrshire, Scotland
> On 3 July 1364 he had charters from teh 9th Earl of Mar of the lands of Edinbanchory and Craiglogy, which was confirmed by King DAvid II. He held the office of Sheriff of Aberdeen in 1374. On 18 July 1378 he was granted the lands of Findrassie by the Bishop of Moray.

Margaret Lord

> Birth 1311 in Forbes, Aberdeenshire, Scotland
> Death 29 Sep 1349 in Islands, Orkney, Scotland

Margaret's parents were John Lord (1270-1300) and Joan DeFiennes (1272-1309). John Lord was from Northamptonshire, England.

GENERATION TWENTY

Alexander DeForbes (1286-1332) and _____ (1290-1350)

    Birth 1286 in Dublin, Dublin, Ireland
    Death 1332 in Dublin, Dublin, Ireland

GENERATION TWENTY-ONE

Alexander DeForbes (1256-1304) and _____ (1256-)

    Birth 1256 in Forbes, Aberdeenshire, Scotland
    Death 1304 in Murray, Scotland

GENERATION TWENTY-TWO

Ferglx DeForbes (1226-1272) and _____ (1230-)

    Birth 1226 in Forbes, Aberdeenshire, Scotland
    Death 1272

GENERATION TWENTY-THREE

John DeForbes (1176-1225) and _____ (1180-)

    Birth 1176 in Forbes, Aberdeenshire, Scotland
    Death 1225 in Forbes, Aberdeenshire, Scotland

GENERATION TWENTY-FOUR

Duncan Forbois (1120-1177)

> Birth 1120 in Forbes, Aberdeenshire, Scotland
> Death 1177 in Scotland

Scotland THE FORBESES. 291 To commemorate his having killed the bear for "Bess." Another tradition states that the name of the founder of the family was originally Bois, a follower of an early Scottish king, and that on granting him certain lands for some extraordinary' service, his majesty observed that they were " for boice." The surname, however, is territorial, and said to be Celtic, from the Gaelic word Ferbash or Ferbasach, a bold man.

" On the whole," says Smibcrt, " the traditions of the family, as well as other authorities, countenance with unusual strength, the belief, that the **heads of the Forbeses belonged really to the Irish branch**, and were among those strangers of that race whom the Lowland kings planted in the north and north-east of Scotland to orerawc the remaining primary population of Gaelic Picts."

According to Skene, in his treatise **De Verhorum Significatione, Duncan Forbois** got from King Alexander (but which of the three Kings of that name is not mentioned) a charter of the lands and heritage of Forbois in Aberdeenshire, whence the surname. In the reign of King William the Lion, John de Forbes possessed the lands of that name. His son, Fergus de Forbes, had a charter of the same from Alexander, lord of Buchan, about 1236. Next of this race are Duncan de Forbes, his son, 1262, and Alexander de Forbes, grandson, governor of Urcpdiart Castle in Moray, which he bravely defended for a long time, in 1304, against Edward I, of England; but on its surrender all within the castle were put to the sword, except the wife of the governor, who escaped to Ireland, and was there delivered of a posthumous son. This son, Sir Alexander de Forbes, the only one of his family remaining, came to Scotland in the reign of Robert the Bruce, and his patrimonial inheritance of Forlx's having seen bestowed upon others, obtained a government of other lands instead. He was killed at the battle of Duplin, in 1332, fighting valiantly on the side of King David, he son of Bruce. From his son, Sir John de Forbes, 1373, all the numerous families in Scotland who bear the name and their offspring, their descent.

GENERATION TWENTY-FIVE

Ochonacar Forbois (1100-1158)

> Birth 1100 in Aberdeenshire, Scotland
> Death 1158 in Aberdeenshire, Scotland

GENERATION TWENTY-SIX

Chevalier Adam Forbois (1075-1100)

> Birth 1075 in Aberdeenshire, Scotland
> Death 1100 in Scotland

FORBES CASTLE

Castle Forbes is a 19th-century country house near Alford in Aberdeenshire, Scotland.

The estate is over 6,000 acres and has been in the Forbes family for over 600 years. The original house was named Putachie. The present castle overlooking the River Don was built in 1815 by the 17th Lord Forbes, to designs by the architect Archibald Simpson. However, after Simpson encountered structural problems and the original section of the house (from c. 1731) began to crack, Simpson was dismissed and the work was completed by the City Architect of Aberdeen, John Smith.

Today it is occupied by Malcolm Forbes, 23rd Lord Forbes and his wife Jinny and open to residential guests.

There is a stone circle dating to 3000 BC on the estate.

ANOTHER FORBES HOUSE

The Culloden House is a beautiful hotel in Inverness.   It was once owned by the Forbes of Culloden from 1626 to 1897. At that time there was a square renaissance building but it burned down.   This house is from 1772.   Bonnie Prince Charles stayed here just before the Battle of Cullorden.

I actually stayed here for two nights on a recent vacation to Scotland and never knew I was related to this Forbes family. I do remember the secret walled garden they have on the propety which is beautiful and full of flowers and greenery. There was a sign on the gate about it being created by the Forbes family.

Druminnor Castle

On the banks of the burn of Keron, in a sloping steep valley two miles east of Rynie in Aberdeen-shire, possibly the original Castle Forbes of the Aberdeen-shire Forbeses, pre-dating by centuries the present Castle Forbes. A still older castle further up the Don River existed from 1271 as a result of a grant of land to Duncan Forbes made by King Alexander III. This third Druminnor was built between 1440-1470 and was originally a rectangular block attached to the second tower. The tower house of the 1450s was completely demolished early in the 19th century. The doorway arch of the castle, made of five straight sections, is probably unique in Scotland. The heavy corbelling which carries the circular stair tower squared out to provide the watch-room above three Forbes crests, dates from 1577. The castle suffered many tribulations over the years but was finally rescued and restored by the late Honorable Margaret Forbes-Semphill. All the basements are vaulted. The first floor has a superb Great Hall, in which it was said that fifteen Gordons were murdered by Forbes men during a banquet in 1571, after the latest bout of the protracted Clan feud. It was also from this castle that the battle of Tillyangus occured between the Forbeses and Gordons after the Master of Forbes repudiated his wife who was the daughter of the Earl of Huntly. Black Arthur, the brother of Lord Forbes, was killed by William Gordon of

Terpersie and the victorious Gordons chased the fleeing Forbes right up to the gates of Druminnor Castle.

YESTER CASTLE

Is now in ruins but this is what it looked like in the day. See notes above for Yester castle. This is where Lady Mary Douglas died.

DIFFERENT BRANCHES OF THE FORBES CLAN IN SCOTLAND

Branches of the Forbes Clan

 Mostly in Aberdeenshire, are or were the Forbes of Balfluig; Forbes of Belnabodach; Forbes of Boyndlie; Forbes of Brux; Forbes of Callendar; Forbes of Castleton, Forbes of Corse, Forbes of Corsindae, Forbes of Craigievar, Forbes of Culloden (see "Culloden House"), Forbes of Culquhonny, Forbes of Echt, Forbes of Foveran, Forbes of Invernan, Forbes of Kildrummy,

Forbes of Ledmacoy, Forbes of Leslie, Forbes of Monymusk, Forbes of Newe, Forbes of Newtownforbes (Eire), Forbes of Pitnacalder, Forbes of Pitsligo, Forbes of Rothiemay, Forbes of Thainston, Forbes of Tolquhoun, Forbes of Towie, Forbes of Waterton.

FAMILY NOTES:

www.ingramcontent.com/pod-product-compliance
Lightning Source LLC
Chambersburg PA
CBHW050754290526
45792CB00008B/2183